THE GENRE OF SILENCE

THE GENRE OF SILENCE

DUNCAN BUSH

Illustrated by John Selway

Seren is the book imprint of
Poetry Wales Press Ltd
Nolton Street, Bridgend, Wales

**Explore thirty years of Seren books at
www.serenbooks.com**

Text © Duncan Bush, 1988
Images © John Selway, 1988

Reprinted 2011

The right of Duncan Bush to be identified
as the Author of this Work has been asserted
in accordance with the Copyright, Designs
and Patents Act, 1988.

ISBN 978-0-907476-90-0

A CIP record for this title is available from
the British Library

All rights reserved. No part of this publication
may be reproduced, stored in a retrieval system,
or transmitted at any time or by any means
electronic, mechanical, photocopying, recording
or otherwise without the prior permission
of the copyright holder.

The publisher works with the financial assistance
of the Welsh Books Council

Printed by Harcourt Colourprint, Swansea

CONTENTS

IN THE PINE FOREST   9

1. THE SURVIVING POEMS OF VICTOR BAL

Poems from the Civil War Years
Black Smoke	17
Archaic Profile	19
Toy Soldier	23
Peasant Burial	24
Peasant	27

Poems from the Stalin Years
Writers' Union Building, Moscow, 1937	31
The Leader	32
For Osip Emilievich Mandelstam	33
For Isaac Emanuelovich Babel	35
The Age of Rust	37
Night, Day	38

Appendix: Early Poems
Galley	43
Summer, Evening	45
For Marina	47

2. HOW IT WAS

1. A Brief Life	51
2. Gubski's Hatbox	54
3. The Last Doll	56
4. In the Ukraine	66
5. Endgame	68
6. An Education in the Classics	71
7. Russian Roulette	73
8. How It Was Done in the Don Basin	75
9. Internal Exile of the Houseplant	78

10. Stalin's Wings	82
11. Mandelstam's Bird	84
12. The Moscow Reckoning	88
13. Editorial Reminiscences	94
14. Vronsky's Toothache	98
All the Scattered Fragments	100

Everything is known, but much has been forgotten
— Gabriel Garcia Márquez

In the Pine Forest

In May 1938 two men stood at the fringe of a pinewood near a village to the east of the Ural Mountains. They were trimming the tops and branches off felled conifers with a big two-man bow-saw. It was a fine spring day — the warmest of the year so far — and they took so much pleasure in the exercise and open air that they sometimes made a joke of the very labour of sawing, each trying to set a pace impossible for the other, so that invariably they sawed down crosswise through the trunk with an intense grin on their faces and then fell back exhausted, with relieved laughter, as the last saw-stroke broke through and the offcut fell to the ground.

Gregory Vershinin was tall and well-built, an engineer, who had been a rower in his youth. His companion was Victor Bal, a sallow, stocky man who had once happened to say he was a poet. Vershinin had laughed and said that being a poet wasn't a job. Bal had replied with a kind of mocking gravity that it was worse than that, because you could always change your job but being a poet was sometimes an inescapable fact of identity, like being a Georgian or a Jew. And then in a way that signalled the obviousness of the ploy, he'd changed the subject.

"Right," said Vershinin. "Let's stop all this clowning around and use the damn saw properly. If we snap this blade, Christ knows where we'll get another one."

His right shoulder already felt tired. It would be stiff tonight and ache tomorrow. His muscles weren't used to this. And they weren't what they had been.

"Anyway," he said. "We're going at it too fast, if we want to last the day out."

Bal sat down on one of the old stumps. "I could do with a drink of water," he said.

"Rhythm," Vershinin said. "That's the secret of sawing. If you can get a rhythm going between you, then it's easy. Like fucking your old lady." Bal grimaced faintly and looked away.

Vershinin sat on a stump and made a cigarette. You felt like a free man on a day like this, making a nice thin cigarette and then watching the smoke come out of your mouth in the sunlight.

"The spring's early this year," he observed.

He had been here longer than Bal, and frequently invoked present conditions – of climate, accommodation, or availability of foodstuffs on –

some scale of judicious comparison with the past.

"This time last year the sap was still frozen solid in the trees," he said.

Bal looked at the fresh-cut tree stump in front of him, leaned forward and touched it to see how tacky it was.

"I know," he said. "You only had to put a cup of hot tea down for a minute and there'd be a film of ice across it when you went to pick it up. And this was in your room. Life was hard out here in those days."

He threw an ironic sidelong glance towards Vershinin, to show there was no malice in the ridicule. Then he yawned and leaned forward again, resting his back. Suppressing another yawn, he blinked once or twice, somnolently, at the moist, somehow startlingly white disc of the just-felled tree. Earlier, he had tried counting the rings in one of the bigger trees they had cut down, but they were too close together: your eye lost track of where it was, and you had to keep starting again.

Bal took his one mitten off as Vershinin passed him the pinched butt of the cigarette. He inhaled deeply. Sometimes – like now – a cigarette out here made your head swim, like the first cigarette you ever smoked.

"Don't burn your moustache off," Vershinin said drily, anxious for the last drag. He could never understand, given Bal's views, why he still had that thick, black moustache, like the man in the posters. He'd said this to Bal once, who had smiled thinly. "I had this moustache," he said, "before I ever heard of him, let alone saw his picture. I wouldn't pull a grey hair out of my head because of that bastard. Let alone shave off a black moustache."

"Yes," Bal said. "It does seem early this year."

He looked away from the dark fir-woods, across the wasteground of old stumps. He was trying to write a poem – or rather, to memorise what he had of it in his head so far – and Vershinin was distracting him.

Earlier, Bal had gone into the fir-woods for a shit and, looking for a branch of the right height to sit over – he couldn't squat down because of his stiff knee: a wound from the Civil War of twenty years ago – had gone so deep into that darkening silence that when he looked back he could barely see the windows of white daylight between the trunks at the edge of the wood. He had left a little pile of turds smoking at the foot of one of the trees. There was blood in them again. And, as he buttoned his trousers and walked back towards the fringed daylight, on that soundless floor of brown needles, the first line of his poem came to him, which compared the silence of the Russia of that time to the immense, ominous silence there is in its pine forests.

"That means we'll be getting the mosquitoes sooner," said Vershinin. He nodded pedantically, again in that way he had of imparting everything he had learned out here like immemorial lore.

Bal gave up on the poem for now. The movement of the first line wasn't quite right yet. Rhythm was the secret of more than just sawing or fucking your old lady. But hold on to that first line, that was the thing. Let the rest of it work quietly within you, like a bulb in the earth. Though, if you thought about it, what was the point, finally, in writing poems the bastards would never let you publish? That, of course, was what the poem was all about. A paradox. A poem that bespoke its own impossibility.

"Yes," he answered.

He yawned again.

"I saw a butterfly yesterday."

"What?"

Vershinin's pale eyes squinted at him doubtfully, as if in his experience this was unthinkable so early in the year.

"I think I did." Bal shrugged. "Either that or I dreamed it," he said. "A big white one. Like a formal dress bow-tie I had once, in the bad old days." He laughed.

"I suppose that's a typical example of modern poetry, is it?" said Vershinin, who enjoyed playing the sceptic and philistine in Bal's company. "You've got to compare something natural, like a butterfly, to something unnatural, like a bow-tie. Why not do it the other way round, and compare the bow-tie to the butterfly? Now that would be alright."

Bal shrugged. "I don't know," he said. "These are unnatural times."

"Fucking poets," said Vershinin, trying to needle Bal in the usual way. "What this revolution needs" – he flourished a fist – "is workers, not poets."

"What this revolution needs is revolutionaries," said Bal.

"Poets," said Vershinin, unable to leave it alone. "Parasites. Only one thing to do with you lot."

"And what's that?"

"Take you out and fucking shoot you."

Vershinin laughed in delight at Bal's pained expression over this new instance of barbarism. Bal smiled faintly, pityingly at his friend, and shook his head. He handed back the stained butt of the cigarette.

"We'd better get back to work," he said.

He looked to his right, where another pair of men was working on the line of trees. The bone-litter of old branches, probably cut last year *or the year before that, had already lost their bark and weathered to a grained silvery sheen in the sunlight. He let the first line of the poem run once more through his head before he stood up after Vershinin.*

The next day Bal was to finish the poem, and write it out in his notebook. Then, that evening, he read it aloud to Vershinin, who sat in silence for a long time afterwards. Then he asked Bal to read the poem again. Then Vershinin shook his head, and looked at his friend.

"I couldn't have written anything like that," he said. "Not in a million years."

Much later someone else would read the poem too, someone who unlike Vershinin only needed to read it once to know what it was saying. And then the poem about the pine forest disappeared, like the man who had written it.

1. THE SURVIVING POEMS OF VICTOR BAL

Poems
from the Civil War Years

Black Smoke

Black smoke of fires we set or see
are not for burning stubble.
Across the ravaged chessboard
of the Ukraine wheatfields

we give chase or flee.
Greek potters saw it
first: the hunter turning
into quarry in the rotation

of a vase. What we come upon
or leave are dead and dying.
And only in mythology
can Daphne change into the tree.

Archaic Profile

Bessmanov was shot in the nose last week.
A White bullet took away most of
the fleshy tip, leaving the bone
undamaged. Four inches to the right,

it would have gone into one ear
and out the other before
he heard the flat crack
of the rifle. One inch to the left,

it would have missed him altogether.
Who can explain these things?
And why try, when death already
chafes us no more than an old boot?

A handsome, quiet youth
he was, Bessmanov, who probably
hardly even knew about the odd heart
he must have stirred out in

whatever poor, far-flung paltry villages
were the total sum of his
experience before he saw the war.
Now the war is all there is.

And with those squalid strips of
bandaging taped down the bridge of
where his nose was and below the eyes,
suddenly he has attained

a fearsome look of martial savagery:
the nasal prow and cheek-pieces
of some bronze-green, ancient
helmet. So much for the classic sense.

The best that Bessmanov will hope for now
is not to lose his nose in one corner
of the Ukraine and his body,
six weeks later, in another.

And when the war is over and those
filthy dressings off, if he goes home
at last in his Red Army
uniform, with polished boots,

his bandaged, minatory stare grown mild,
will women ever again begin to see him
as, for a moment then, I almost did:
like the archaic torsoes of Greek heroes

– Zeus, say, or Odysseus –
with their blank, far-seeing eyes,
blond marble curls, and
that terrible, noseless beauty?

Toy Soldier

On his son's birthday Strelkov
melted down bullets on the sly
to cast a toy soldier
in a mould he'd carved.

Blunt bullets, dull lead
bright as quicksilver in the old
smoke-black tin he used to pour.
Dolgushin turned his back

in an asthma of contempt, blinking
fiercely at the steppe, a universe
of scarcity. He was right.
They're my bullets, Strelkov said.

He laughed foolishly, for us.
Not fucking yours. And he was right.
It's such a light thing, life.
Less than a frosty breath.

You weigh five bullets
in your hand before you load,
and it's all you've got,
and each of them is a life.

But to move a man dead
is to wrestle
a sack of stones
across rough ground.

Peasant Burial

The mountains are white and black
like outpinned wings of
some great silent snowy owl
that came on this wind out of the Arctic.

Here, only just can the earth
still be dug for a grave.
Through the pointless wailing
of the women, the second-born is borne

in a child's small coffin
in her brother's washed white nightdress
still and now forever too big for her.
And the wind's enough to make you cry.

Peasant

You are the hand's roughness,
and the polish
on the haft of each tool.
And you are the sullen

cunning in that blue eye
hooded now, and the dark centuries
of Russia still hard in you,
and the old brutalisms –

like the Party official
with his belly slit open
and stuffed with grain, with grain
and blind maggots, we found

left on the roadside as a sign.

Poems
from the Stalin Years

Writers' Union Building, Moscow, 1937

Free hotel? Or tomb of living writers?
Even the labradorite entrance
betrays a funebral air of pomp.

Though for some these numbered floors rise
sheer as a fiery Jacob's ladder,
each lift's a greasy pole.

This year, they tell me, members are
sporting Ukrainian embroidered shirts
when they herd to conferences –

sheep in peasant's clothing. Sheep
milling for the microphone
like wolves. And, like wolves, getting

stronger the longer you run.

The Leader

Fabulous beast, father, in our dreams we
wonder sometimes if you really do
exist. One gives you six legs
like an insect, or a thousand like

a battalion. Another, a dragonfly's
wings, and an ant-coloured
Assyrian beard; and in your plaited
beehive hat, a multitude of

layered cells, more rooms than
the Palace of Soviets or the Hotel Moskva,
each one a perfect hexagon.
That swarming is

your thoughts. But, like everyone, I
must think I dream you as
you truly are: seeing you always
on a medal round your own neck, but

ubiquitous as coin: half-profiled
bas-relief of bronze stone gazing right,
shrewd-eyed into the future, the future
some of us won't see.

For Osip Emilievich Mandelstam

Mandelstam, poor Mandelstam.
A hunger, like the rest of us,
for drabbest domesticity, all
you wanted sometimes was
to be your goldfinch:
a little millet seed, a change
of newspaper, some water
and a hooded cloth at night...
Safer, you thought, in days
like these, to live a bird
than as a man,
pretending to forget that
cagebirds sing, and can be heard.

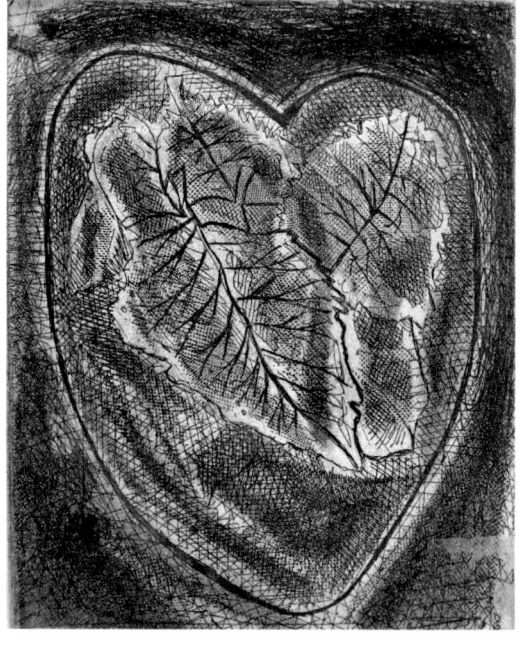

For Isaac Emanuelovich Babel

Babel's typewriter is silence now,
himself the originator of that genre,
as he said. No steel, he wrote
once, enters the heart with surer violence

than a full stop in the right place –
though a point of prose style
was what he had in mind
that time. The ultimate Punctuation Mark

we may be sure he always knew about:
two years with the Red Cavalry
across the nowhere-ending plains,
then fighting for his life

at the Writers' Congress from a podium ...
He was, perhaps, the best of us.
He knew what he had seen
in the Palace of Motherhood,

the leaden-faced, one-pound-weight baby of
some poor slut out of Moscow's wooden slums
a candleflame of life cupped
by the Revolution's clumsy hands.

Best of all, though, perhaps he
understood, that day
in the Jewish cemetery
at Kozin, the old words cut into

stone the green of stagnant ponds:
O death, o covetous one, o greedy thief,
why couldst thou not
have spared us just for once?

And when I think of this
I think of the bullet
someone surely carries
for this Odessan Jewish boy

with nickel-rimmed spectacles on his nose
and autumn in his heart –
carries for the space between
those high, wide temples.

The Age of Rust

*... quiet labour makes the iron plough gleam,
and the poet's voice.*
— Mandelstam

    We lost our adolescent voices
    in the garrulity and

    self-promotion of the cenacles.
    Our adult voice broke

    to a wheedle on the times'
    skullduggery and paranoia. Now

    we know only those words
    persist which are self-seeding,

    perennial, unkillable as thistle
    or the slow green fire

    of couch grass licking
    out of winter's straw.

    As leafy shoots one year are
    noticed to have sprung

    sheafed thick as arrows
    round the target of

    a cut-back stump.

Night, Day

We lie awake at night and dream
the knocking at the door through which
we'll disappear for ever. By day, commune
our fate and share deliverance with

surprising crowds left on the pavements still.
By the Kremlin wall, too, a queue lengthens
in patience, as if to view
the calf's blood and pig's bones

of Christ. While with every swivel-perfect
change of guard, even Lenin,
waxen in the mausolem, thinks
that they have come for him at last.

Appendix:
Early Poems

The Galley

Let some have whips and wear uniform.
Let some have oars and wear rag. Let these
be more. So have them shackled
at ankle and wrist. Let the galley

move. The immense effort of shifting
inert mass through sea is well known.
A strange thing is, those
in the uniform think it's the strokes

of the whip which achieve it.

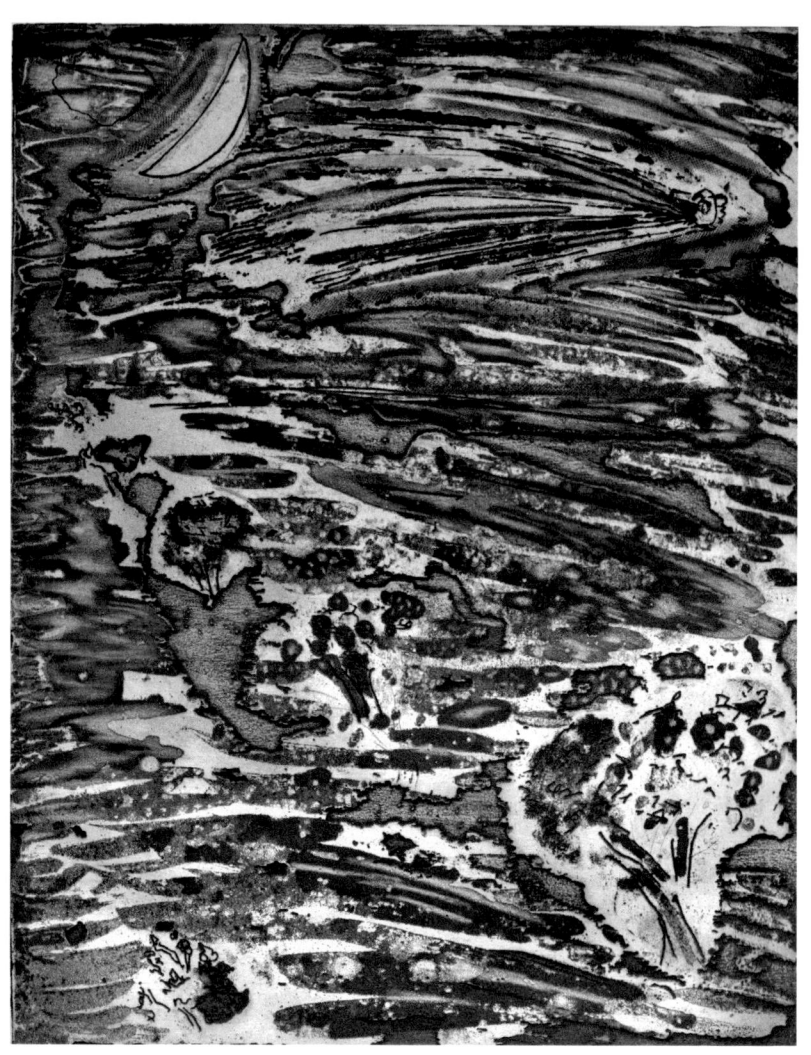

Summer, Evening

Early evening. West, a
single, white cloud

high in pale summer
sky. A June sky so

summer-pale, so high,
a cloud so small, so

singular, that it's as
if you've known this all

before, it may have
been years ago, perhaps

in adolescence, and
like the great comet

looping space, or
a forgotten anniversary,

it has simply rotated
round again at last

as on an orrery. And you
realise that the most

there is is that
you'll die and

always it will all be
as it was before:

Evening. Summer sky.
A single cloud. A boy

wandering the pathway
of a city park

towards hawthorns
bridal with, aburn

with blossom.

For Marina

I love the way your big toes point
down the bed when you come –

most of all in summer, when again
we can lie on, not under,

the strawberry-flowered quilt
in the full afternoon

naked as the new-born
mice under the floorboarding

we couldn't bring ourselves
to poison, and as blind

to everything except
each other's bodies,

yours so long and beautiful
sometimes it hurts my heart

and makes my eyes
flinch almost so I have to look

away, as from a mirror
flashing all the sun into my face.

2. HOW IT WAS

1

A Brief Life

Victor Bal was born on January 3, 1898, in the Kolomna district of Petersburg. The son of a doctor, he attended the Tenishev School (as Mandelstam and Nabokov had, a few years earlier). Bal was a student at Petersburg University when the October Revolution took place in 1917. He seems not to have completed his studies, for in 1918 he enlisted on the side of the Reds in the Civil War. In 1920 he received a wound in the knee, which led to his discharge. Returning to Petersburg (now Petrograd), he worked on a journal, then moved to Moscow, to work on film scripts. He also wrote poetry, and in 1922, at his own expense, published the collection *Sunflowers*, which gained little notice. Bal married Marina Ivanovna Rostova in 1924.

Little is known of Bal's life or work over the subsequent decade and beyond: "History is a sieve that picks up only a small proportion of the debris of the past. What it salvages is, above all, books and manuscripts. But, as Goethe put it, 'of what has been done and said only a tiny part has been remembered.' What is honoured as literature is a 'fragment of fragments' ".

As it happens, these words of Theodore Zeidin's were written of France in the nineteenth century. They are true of all countries in all periods. But they were never more applicable than to the Soviet Union at this time, which was about to enter a period of personal upheaval, cultural repression and instantaneous historical amnesia: a chronic and all-pervasive atmosphere, in every aspect of daily life, of what one of Bal's own poems, with massive understatement, refers to as "the times' skullduggery and paranoia".

It is in this period, following the death of Lenin in January 1924, that the Revolutionary process (which Bal, along with many other intellectuals, had supported) enters its most critical phase. A struggle for the succession begins, from which, by the end of the decade, Stalin will emerge in absolute control. Trotsky is expelled from the Party. The 'right wing' opposition, led by Bukharin, is defeated, an outcome which is to culminate in the Moscow trials. On the literary front, an equally fierce struggle is being fought between the literary conservatives and LEF (Left Front of Art), founded by Mayakovsky, Khlebnikov, Asayev, Brik, and other writers. The poet Yesenin commits suicide. His last lines are written in his own venous blood: "In this life there's nothing new about dying. But there's nothing new about living either." Lenin's New Economic Policy (NEP) comes to an end and Stalin's first Five Year Plan for the rapid industrialisation of the whole country is announced. LEF ceases to exist. RAPP (The Association of 'Proletarian Writers') mounts a vehement campaign against 'uncommitted' writers and 'fellow travellers'. Trotsky is exiled. Mayakovsky shoots himself through the heart with a Browning revolver. Gorky is driven around Moscow alone in the back seat of a big blue Lincoln car. In the countryside, collectivisation is stepped up. The peasants burn the crop and slaughter their own livestock rather than have it fall into the hands of the State. RAPP is dissolved. Mass deportation of the kulaks takes place. There is widespread famine in the countryside and severe rationing of foodstuffs in the towns and cities. A privilege system of special rations and closed 'shops' is introduced for certain favoured writers and intellectuals.

1934 sees the First Congress of the Writers' Union, now firmly under State Control, and the commencement of political terror.

In the summer and autumn of 1937 Bal has several meetings or interviews in Leningrad with the critic Y.N. Gubski, who seems to be collecting material for an article or monograph on Bal's work. Later in the same year Bal is exiled to the Urals. It is at this time that Yagoda, head of the Secret Police, is dismissed by Stalin for 'liberalism', and replaced by Yezhov, the 'Bloodthirsty Dwarf'. The *Yezhovshchina* or Great Terror begins: thousands are executed, millions arrested and deported to concentration camps. Among those who 'disappear' are intellectuals, Red Army leaders and former revolutionaries. Also, an inestimable number of ordinary people whose names, even now, are known for the most part only to their families, and the circumstances of their deaths not at all. For these individuals, the coincidence in a surname, an overheard remark, or the malicious report of a single neighbour, colleague or workmate, may have been enough. As common speech puts it: "For every man there's another to watch him". Over the next decade of Stalin's rule, among those groups most systematically subjected to repression, arrest, imprisonment and death are writers.

Ehrenburg was to calculate later that of the 700 writers present at the First Writers' Congress in 1934, only 50 survived to see the Second in 1954. In the words of Nadezhda Mandelstam, with the example of her own husband in mind: "People can be killed for poetry here – a sign of unparalleled respect – because they are still capable of living by it".

From the spring of 1938, nothing is known of the whereabouts or eventual fate of Victor Bal.

2

Gubski's Hatbox

The unpublished poems of Victor Bal were found, in a banded leather hatbox, among the papers of the critic and minor poet Yevgeni Nikolayevich Gubski. After Gubski's suicide in 1954 they were kept by his daughter N.Y. Surkova until her own death in 1986, when another member of the family made them available to the editor L.V. Slavnikov. Together with Bal's poems were extracts, in Gubski's hand, from transcripts of the interviews or conversations which Gubski had with Bal in the latter part of 1937. There were also several incomplete drafts of poems by Bal, the beginning of a prose autobiography, and some pages of what appear to be sections torn from Bal's notebooks from the Civil War years, when Bal was with the Red Army in the Ukraine. The complete journal or journals, which would have been of great interest, have never been found. The only extracts from the interviews or of Bal's journals that Gubski seems to have been interested to preserve relate in the main to the poems themselves.

In the Notes which follow, use has been made of additional material referred to above, for clarification of a notably murky period and to furnish a general cultural or historical background to the poems. On the same principle, some of Bal's poems in draft have been incorporated into these Notes rather than published in the main body of the text, in keeping with what (as will be seen from Gubski's records of their meetings) seem to have been Bal's views on his own 'unfinished' or 'abandoned' poems.

Gubski's own literary career was an unsuccessful one, and his later life was marked with periodic mental unbalance. After Bal's presumed death Gubski is said to have taken an intensely secretive and proprietorial attitude to the poems of Bal's that were in his possession, one of the early examples of which ('The Galley') he attempted to publish as his own. At the head of one of Bal's manuscript pages he wrote: "I'm the mother of these poems now. As a farmyard dog can be mother to a whole string of ducklings".

Perhaps it is this rather sad example of posthumous plagiarism which has given rise to the suggestion that Bal's second period of internal exile in November 1937 came about as a result of his betrayal by Gubski, following their meetings in the summer and autumn of that year: that several of Bal's poems, or certain remarks he may have uttered in Gubski's presence, were made known to the authorities. However, the only certain thing is that this possibility will never now be proved. It is futile, therefore, to add the fuel of suppositional hindsight to an age that already smouldered with damaging, and often fatal, rumour. In view of Gubski's subsequent instability, it may certainly be argued that it was unfortunate, if not inexplicable, that Bal trusted him with this material in the first place. But is it clear from the poems that Bal could already sense the probable future, and perhaps no other literary confidant or executor was available to him. Not every writer marries a Nadezhda Mandelstam (Bal and his wife Marina were divorced in 1934, after several years of separation). As Bal subsequently was to write, in another ink, on one of his own manuscripts: "These days poems don't belong in bookshops or on shelves, but under the carpet or, best of all, in the stove".

It may be worth recording that when all of the literary material mentioned above had been taken out for examination, also in the box was found a single sunflower seed: black-and-white striped, like a tiny humbug. Had Bal brought it as an ironic token for Gubski on his first visit? (Bal's 1922 collection of poems *Sunflowers* – like Pasternak's play *Blind Beauty*, Gorki's last notebooks, or the unnumbered unknown works of innumerable unknown others – has not reached the eyes of posterity.)

In August 1954 Yevgeni Nikolayevich Gubski, who was a tall man, removed three screws from the plate of a coathook on the back of his study door, and then stood on the arm of a chair to screw the coathook to a wooden ceiling joist. He then hanged himself from it, using the cord of the dressing-gown he was wearing, and underneath which he was naked. In one of the pockets was found the screwdriver. In the other was a note, which read: "A last erection. Impotence all my life till now. Joining the pointless dead, who outnumber the living as worms outnumber birds".

In all of this, one indisputable fact is that but for Gubski's hatbox we should know far less of Bal and of his works that we now do.

3

The Last Doll

(from *A Kolomna Year* – sections from a prose autobiography by Victor Bal)

After each winter of green goose-grease scarves, one or other of the old people would have died. This is what I find I remember now. Every winter one more would have died, and yet their number never grew less. The apparently unchanging numerousness of my assortment of relations – uncles, aunts, great aunts, great uncles, cousins of my parents, cousins of their cousins, and so on – gave, it has always seemed to me, particular meaning to the term 'extended family'; at least, so far as it applied to the Kolomna District. To speak geographically rather than genealogically, however, in the Kolomna 'extended' meant no further than the corner before the Mariinski, and was usually a good deal closer. Moreover, there was invariably one, sometimes two, of our relatives residing with us in our house near the corner of Pskov Street and Lotzman Street. Children are not conscious of linear time, and either forget or have already accepted as permanent what they only intermittently see. But I can now understand that our visitors must have sometimes stayed weeks, or even months, from that single expressive but hopeless glance I remember my father once throwing upward at the ceiling through which Uncle Shura could be heard pacing, waiting for his summons down to supper.

    Uncle Shura stayed with us almost a year, it turns out. He had had a florist's business, but all that remained of this now was the creamy-white chrysanthemum he sometimes returned with in his lapel. Occasionally, when he thought to do so, he would present this bloom to my mother with an ironic flourish. She would sniff it a little haughtily (though hauteur was not convincing in my mother), and put it aside; later, she would nevertheless slit the stalk to help it 'keep', and stand it on the shelf of the mantelpiece in a tiny vase of water that must have been specifically made for buttonholes. There, it gradually snowed a litter of brownish petals until someone thought to sweep them into the hand and throw them, with the dead stalk, into the fire. This neglect was unusual, as my mother loved fresh flowers in the house, and changed them and their water regularly. I now understand that my mother only consented to accept this flower because she did not have the heart to completely refuse either Uncle Shura or such a beautiful chrysanthemum. But, like the first sniff, her subsequent neglect of the periodically-reappearing white buttonhole conveyed her unhappiness at the knowledge as to where my Uncle Shura had just returned from, wearing it. It was only much later, after he had left us, that I heard rumours about his broken marriage, though I never did understand exactly why, or over whom, Aunt Valentina had thrown him out – possibly because that gossip was displaced, as it were, by the other word I came to overhear of him, with an even grimmer emphasis: 'bankrupt'.

'An educated man', as he liked to think (and often said), Uncle Shura was sufficiently sensitive both in himself and of his circumstances not only to act as if there was no suspicion in his mind of the imposition and expense he might be to my father, but even, by taking this blithe pretence of normality a little further, to lord it casually over the family as if he were not so much guest, nor even tenant, in the house but rightful landlord. In time he even took it upon himself to correct the table manners of the children.

Aunt Lidia, on the other hand, stayed longer, but, as my father said, "Lidia's as good as gold. You never notice her." Which, I suppose now, means that she did not contradict him. She contradicted no one. She lived in silence and timorousness somewhere behind the skirting-board in her tiny room, and even had the small and delicate fingers of a mouse, except that she was harder to catch a glimpse of, ate less, and more guiltily. Around her neck, even indoors, she wore a flea-bitten 'sable' – referred to jocularly by my father as "the polecat" – whose glass eyes still held, for me, a baleful and predatory lustre. She wore an amber brooch, in which either memory or imagination has now firmly imprisoned a tiny fly. A black chandelier of jet clicked and tinkled about her when she moved, which was rarely, and little. She had a quality of fearful stillness, which she lost only in death, when those delicate fingers, now locked upon her chest, had finally stopped their ceaseless and unconscious fidgeting with each other, as if rolling away an ear of corn.

That is how I knew she was dead, as I was not so much taken into the room in which she lay as handed quickly through it. I was seven.

Aunt Lidia, probably because I was a favourite of hers, was the first of the old people who had not, so far as I was given to understand, simply 'gone away', ceased to be there in the house. She was there still, but she wasn't, as it seemed. There was that different stillness, her horizontality, the candles and the astonishing and unsuspected length of her hair, which had been brushed out past her waist. There was also, it now seems to me, in a retrospect that perhaps is only half reinvention of the scene, a freezing cold in the room that made of everybody's breath but hers plumes as long and large as those tossing on the foreheads of the horses, glossy as shoe-leather, which had drawn the catafalque at the unknown but obviously important personage's funeral I had glimpsed once from the pavement, near the Izmailov Bridge; the only difference, naturally, lying in the fact that ours were white.

Yet this, I now realise, was in the last days of 1905. And since my memories of that year of revolution are neither more nor less than those of the seven-year-old I was, it is not impossible that I remember the coldness in a particular room on a particular evening while forgetting almost entirely the wider context in which this temperature occurred: strikes in St Petersburg, tens of thousands of people in the streets, the St Petersburg Soviet surrounded by troops on the night of December 3... (In fact, of these public events, I find that I now recall only the crowds, pressing, pressing, jammed in the streets as before a football match, so to speak; but it is dusk, and the scene has a more processional and torchlit quality – which is again perhaps partly a dramatic stage-effect of memory itself.) As to events in our own house, I have a clear memory of overhearing worried rumours that I now know concerned pogroms being planned by the Black Hundreds, but I have completely omitted to remember anything to do with what must have been an entire winter's anguished domestic discussion about the lack of firewood in the city.

Such cold as I have described in that room, however, certainly contradicted one of my mother's articles of wisdom, which held that it wasn't the winter that killed off old people but the first thaw. This original theory may even have had some scientific cogency to it if was meant to imply that cold was less unhealthy than the ensuing St Petersburg dampness, or to make the nice distinction that what killed the old was not the unremitting months below freezing point but, finally, the sheer exhaustion of surviving for that time, a task for which their energies had been scrupulously, if ironically, calculated to be just enough. However, my mother's sense of these things was, I suspect, less an empirical view than a pessimistic though at bottom deeply sentimental sense of fate, drawing less on medical observation than on a certain kind of climax in melodrama where, in the very moment of deliverance, one's hopes are sardonically dashed. It is unnecessary to speculate as to whether this bitter yet emotional sense of destiny is an attribute of whole races or peoples. Herself often enough the bedside spectator of bereavements that passed me by like trams, my mother as an individual had perhaps simply worn threadbare any sense of pity or terror at the circumstance of someone's death, however tragic: two of her own daughters, my sisters, after all, had died, one after the other, before reaching the age of two. And so, what remained, or rather what she substituted for these discomfiting emotions of grief, may have been something of the vicarious tearfulness and throbbing heart with which an audience responds, in secret joy, not to Aristotelian tragedy but to the bathos of a sentimental play.

I am not being disloyal to my mother in saying this. It was much later that I myself came to understand that there may be no such thing as genuine, heartfelt, unsullied sorrow in the event of another person's death. It is also true that every death you witness, every dead person you see, renders you a little more indifferent to the next one. At school, I could scent death in the reek of formalin in the laboratories: the death of dogfish or frog, born not for the freedom of water but for the pickling fluid of dissection. For me, it was this, rather than puberty, which caused the first pang in the testicles. But the only time you really experience the momentousness of human death – other than in the ultimate sense, that is – is the first time you are in its presence. Which is, precisely, the absence of the person who has died. Thus, for months afterwards I still expected to find Aunt Lidia sitting transfixed with nervousness at the dinner table; I sometimes thought I heard jet rattle softly on the stairs. But when I looked at her as I was whisked through that room in which she lay, what I understood with terrible absoluteness was not only that she was dead but that everybody in that room with her would one day die as well: my mother, my father, my Uncle Shura, despite his brick-red face and gallant's sideburns, my brother Jacob. And, most piteously and terrifyingly and tragically of all, myself.

No death I came to witness afterwards would have the impact of that first. In the smouldering villages of the Ukraine I understood that this is why soldiers in wartime become so quickly, callously indifferent to death. It is partly a matter of the insupportable statistical probability: as if the more dead bodies there are, the more likely are they themselves to become one. A kind of resignation occurs. They can see so many dead and dying, even, that their own deaths become a matter of fatigued indifference.

But to see a dead person for the first time is like the moment when a child first recognises that what he sees in the mirror is himself. And no matter how many times afterwards he goes there to brush his hair or squeeze a pimple or worry if he is handsome to women, he will never recapture that moment of confronting the stranger who he also somehow knows to hold the secret of his own identity.

The spring proper, of course, came long after the fatal first thaw. But if, in my mother's belief, what carried off the old, like a plague over Egypt, was the snow melting in St Petersburg, upon the children among us this omen had a precisely opposite effect. After a long, bitter winter – when the pleasures of skating and of crossing the Neva to school other than by the authorised bridges had long been outweighed by the sheer monotonous, miserable boredom of the cold – the first line of water forming at the edges of snow or ice, the sodden feet from softening slush in the gutters, were what enabled us to hang on, keep going for a little longer, and to imagine on some bitterly bright blue day that a faint warmth was now an admixture of this late February sunlight. False spring or not, the air on these days was like the hoop held up in the circus: you felt like diving through that stretched paper drumskin and, on landing again, doing a forward roll: all of this so quickly that you came up running. Skating in the winter was all very well, but for much of the time outdoors you felt as if you were creeping tentative as an old lady with a brittle hip. By now, running was what you missed.

It was only much later that each springtime came to have the effect on me of a searing poignancy that I now imagine it must have for the very old. It seems to me that, for these, in their last years, every greening tree must be a visionary miracle they never hoped to see (so that, unlike my mother, I would even trace their deaths not to the thaw but to a kind of heartburst of unbearable nostalgia and desire). But to the child the prospect of deliverance, renewal was taken annually for granted, like youth and vigour. Now, it was just a question of waiting. Gradually, irreversibly, the snow would vanish from the roofs in drips of water, even if these at first refroze as icicles at night. Even the hard snow in the areas of shadow would imperceptibly begin to shrink.

These memories are commonplace, no doubt. But to speak more generally, I am not sure whether it is perhaps a sentimentality in me, or an individual feature of my memory processes, or even an index of experiences that not only I but an entire generation have undergone, but, in the aftermath of the struggle for this country which culminated in the Civil War, my childhood seemed daily to be coming closer to me, as in the aged.

★

Perhaps the past itself is like one of those Russian dolls, one doll inside another, which embody a profound belief in the principle of the female, of continuity: within the *babushka* is the mother; within her, the daughter; then the grand-daughter; the great grand-daughter; and so on. The biggest, or most numerous, of these multiple dolls – like the one I remember unpacked in a long, diminishing queue in the window of a shop off Million Street – contain enough generations or, to speak physiologically, enough ovaries and eggs, to account for the history of entire genealogies right back to the dark days of the Middle Ages. But always, in their heart of hearts, their ovary of ovaries, their egg of eggs, is discovered the final, the tiniest, figure, the one who does not twist open to reveal another, the one who is intact with her own secret, which is a secret only postponed by all these successive revelations...

Everyone's past is like this: progressively it opens up in diminishing vistas towards that final, irreducible kernel: oneself as a child: or not even yet a child: a baby.

In my case, the secret sealed within that tiny, last doll is the knowledge of my own death, an irreducible fact that I must certainly have first encountered by way of my Aunt Lidia's. There should be no question of morbidity in this. The problem is universal. Yet it is also the most private thing there is. To speak, as only I can, of myself, it has always seemed to me that within all my acts, and as the final secret of every poem I write or ever wanted to, lies a recession to this final, tiniest doll which, even if it is the lightest of them all to carry with you, is the densest, the most solid.

*

Historians (who think in dates, after all, and fill in only the blank spaces between with words), biographers, and even autobiographers, are accustomed to giving the precise year in which an event they are recording happened. But the child, who may actually be the subject of these narratives, knows very few dates: his birthday, and those of his friends and family; holidays, etc. From whence arises a question: When does the child first become conscious of the impersonal, the *universal* time of the year's numerals? I, for example, know the year 1905 – the year of a failed revolution and of a particular death in my family, as referred to earlier – only from simple arithmetic, because my Aunt Lidia died a few days before my eighth birthday. The first universal, or to speak more accurately, cosmic date I became aware of was the year 1910. This was the year that Halley's famous comet was destined to return, seventy-six years (according to the newspaper and our physics teacher at school) after it had last been witnessed by human sight. I was then twelve. The immense mathematics of all this was explained to me very simply, by my father. Grandfather Lubin had been two years of age when the comet last approached the earth – the year of his birth being 1832. When the comet *next* came, I – born in 1898 – would be eighty-eight, even older than grandfather Lubin was now!

It was sufficient, even then, merely to think of my grandfather, with his pale blue Polish eyes and the smell of liniment and those spectral hands trembling upon the arch of his stick, to doubt that I would ever reach a state of such advanced infirmity. Instead, I thought of the long years that the comet spent travelling, in its immense ellipse, the infinite and interstellar cold beyond sight even of my father's leather-cased German telescope with the milled brass eyepiece and the constant hair across the lens.

*

More on the Civil War, which I limped out of before the end. No cause for a gypsy violinist in this. I am every day grateful for my limp, in point of fact. It might as easily have been gangrene.

Walking not much of a problem, or even dancing. Sitting for a long time is uncomfortable, and riding difficult. But most things you can manage with a stick and the faint grimace of a hero and, if asked, then tell the tale.

All our tumultuous recent history has so far cost me personally is my length of stride.
Everything has changed, and for the better, if not yet absolutely for the best. Etc. (Stress this.)

★

More about Petersburg. Delta city, facing Europe.
   City of stone palaces and water.
   Built on swamp, malaria, a Tsar's whim, and the bones of peasants.

The seasons. More on spring.

Summer. Red geraniums in the greenhouse of our front windows.
   My father's desk. Sunlit glass. Warm glow of red mahogany. He sat with his back to the street, while I have always faced the light to work. (The cross of struts in this window now: lux mea crux.) The concealed drawer in which he kept pills for his migraine. Third in all St Petersburg in his final matriculation from the Medical School.
   The brass mechanism which reduced the movement of the planets about the sun to clockwork.
   The calf *Anatomy* with its plates of flayed corpses. Words like *lymph*, *spleen*, *pancreas*. Red and blue the enchanted circles of the blood, like the lines on the map of the new Moscow subway.

Autumn. Even the trees burning goldest in the Tsar's parks, his estates in the heart of the city.
   Though nothing then that was not his: every birch tree, every owl, every louse or tick upon it, all the way east from the green Gulf of Finland almost to Japan. In my first school one teacher had us learn his titles until we could stand up and recite them at our desks, like a prayer:
   Nicholas the Second, Emperor and Autocrat of All the Russias, Moscow, Kiev, Vladimir, Novgorod; Tsar of Kazan, Tsar of Astrakhan, Tsar of Poland, Tsar of Siberia, Tsar of Tauric Kershon, Tsar of Georgia; Ruler of Pskov and Grand Prince of Smolensk, Lithuania, Volhynia, Podolsk and Finland; Prince of...
   That's all I can remember of it now, but there was another page or so of titles before the whole list was rounded off by *et cetera, et*

cetera. Then, to all this came the solemn vow: *In God and Thee we serve.*

Slower, duller than most of his own peasants, nothing he had ever looked upon he didn't own, or could understand. And all the title and territories, one sixth of the land surface of the planet, no more than the span of a big work-harshened hand across the angled globe I used to spin beside my father's bookshelves.

What was he like, this mild, pale, slow man, with his curled moustaches and vain beard?

It's said that even in the depths of winter, the temperature in every room in his palaces was kept over eighty degrees.

And once, when I worked at the film studio in Moscow, someone ran me a clip of film they'd discovered which the Tsar himself had shot (he was an enthusiastic cameraman). It showed various members of his family pelting each other with snowballs in high summer. There was no snow on the ground. The projectiles, it turns out, were cotton wool.

Perhaps that's what he was like. That's what being Tsar means: you can sweat when others freeze and throw snowballs in August.

And what was *he* like as a child, in his white sailor's suit (the same kind that, fifteen years later, I was dressed in)? What memories did he have?

But there will always be those who sentimentalise the Romanov family.

When I feel pity for him or his family or for his sick son Alexei, I think of the babies I saw in the villages, and of the ten-year-old boy the Whites hanged from a lamp-post in Kiev.

★

More on winter: the books. Beware of what you read in childhood, for that is what you will long for in middle age (to misquote Goethe).

Whatever happened to those fat, ivy-green volumes of Dumas with the red and black print on the title page and the beautiful engraved frontispieces, each covered with a translucent layer of waxed paper?

It was from carefully lifting these protective sheets, to see what (according to the illustration) D'Artagnan or Chicot the Jester or Marguerite de Valois looked like, that I first understood literature to be a subject enjoining reverence. (Many years later I would for the first time uncover a breast with the same tenderness.) In the same way, one only has to re-read the opening paragraph of *The Black Tulip* to re-experience the remorseless, breathless, unstoppable (and, to speak frankly, all but uncontrolled) excitement not only of Dumas' narrative style but – so I must have thought, then, because that, after all, was also the speed one had to read at – of history itself.

Unfortunately, in middle age history is slower and more brutal and more boring than in Dumas *Pere* (though, thanks to the historians, sometimes no less fictional).

*

Childhood, that other age, that personal time, a time *before history*, which still rises up in me, as in a sentimentalist.

Not that I want to return to what was there before. The time before the Revolution is now remote and dead as the light from a star. But even those of us who had to grow up without anaesthetic, chewing the bullet of the revolutionary years, may still have in us, to be expunged or anyway explored, the delusion of the wholeness of our childhoods.

As a man called Kozlov I once talked with, whose life, as he well knew, had been saved by someone sawing off his right leg halfway up the thigh, still sometimes even now cannot believe that this had happened since he can still seem to feel, and even move, his toes.

* * *

[Victor Bal's attempt at the autobiography of his childhood, increasingly fragmentary, breaks off at this point. It is not known whether he ever added more to these apparently finished sections and working notes. However, the increasingly fragmentary nature of the narrative, as well as certain explicit statements or self-reminders ('Everything has changed, and for the better, if not yet for the best. Etc. Stress this.'), might suggest that Bal already begins to experience impossible difficulties in reconciling the need to be honest in these reminiscences with the necessity that, to be published, they be found acceptable.]

4

In the Ukraine

By the later months of 1917 Russia had been exhausted of almost everything but discontent. The First World War had been in progress for three years and the Tsar's generals, showing neither malice nor invention, had already sent millions of fit male Russians to their deaths at the front. Strikes, demonstrations and bread riots were increasingly common in the cities. At a certain moment the restlessness of the people was exactly matched by the mutinousness of the troops, and this was the turning point.

Following the October Revolution, a new war was fought across Russia between revolutionary and counter-revolutionary forces. This struggle, which was to persist until 1921, was particularly savage in the Ukraine, where Victor Bal saw action with the Bolsheviks.

The Civil War began in this region in January 1918 with Bolshevik offensives against Nationalists who had proclaimed Ukrainian independence. Under Muraviev, a former Tsarist officer, the Reds advanced to capture the city of Kiev. The Nationalists, however, signed an agreement with the Germans at Brest-Litovsk, by the terms of which the Ukraine effectively became a German satellite. German and Austrian troops began to occupy the Ukraine. The limited Red forces, no match for an army of professional soldiers, were compelled to withdraw. The Reds were also opposed by cossacks from the Don and Kuban regions. Often of mixed Russian and Turkish blood, the cossacks traditionally formed special regiments in the Tsar's armies and had been accorded privileges and grants of land, which they now feared losing. By another tradition and an intense collective pride – not to mention the ungovernable licence of the times – they were still little more than ruthless bands of brigands, rapists and robbers. The peasants, as they had always been, were the ground underfoot: every advance, retreat or foray had to pass over them. While having old and good reason to resent the Whites and fear the cossacks, because of food requisitions they were equally hostile to the Reds.

To the Bolshevik leaders it became clear from the Ukraine campaign that the survival of the Revolution itself depended on the formation of a well-trained, properly-led and well-equipped army. But in the early part of the Civil War the Red forces faced crises of discipline and morale, as well as severe shortages of food and munitions. This only reflected conditions in the country at large, for throughout the entire period of the Civil War the threat of famine was widespread. Despite the organisation of food commissariats with absolute requisitioning power, thousands died of starvation and malnutrition, particularly in the towns and cities. Trotsky, charged with the creation of the Red Army, recorded that during the Ukraine campaign "anarchy" was prevalent "even in the party ranks". From a military viewpoint, and given the circumstances, this was only to be expected in a hastily-trained conscript army kept continually on the move and engaging not only in sporadic pitched battles but subjected to the prolonged stress of sustaining a ferocious and unremitting guerilla warfare.

Thus, while there was concentrated support for the Reds in the partially industrialised towns and cities of south-eastern Russia, the battle for the countryside, fought across vast steppelands, still had to be won.

A long and merciless struggle for the whole region began.

5

Endgame

As Y.N. Gubski notes in an apostil on the manuscript copy of the poem 'Black Smoke', the idea of battle as a game of chess is "Not at first sight one of Bal's freshest metaphors". Gubski adds, a little pedantically, that it may, however, allude to the fact that Bal carried a travelling chess-set with him for use "in quiet moments, even during the Ukraine campaign", and was a "keen, if moderately gifted, player". (Had Gubski played him and won?)

Gubski possessed several pages of Bal's Notebooks from this period:

> Dec[ember] 17, 1919. Each day gleams empty as our common shaving mirror. High skies, hard light. Most of us have let our beards grow in this terrible wind. Immense weariness at night, simply from being in it all day. But after this last month we're all so tired now even a beard seems an unlikely achievement, like the one a corpse is said to produce. After we took Kiev we thought we'd mop up this whole area in weeks.
>
> "So this is communism, is it?" Khatchikov said the other day. "Or is it just army life? Sharing everything. Always a queue to the same place, whether to shave or shit."
>
> Katchikov has earnt the right to make jokes like that if he wants to. Some laughed. Others nodded. But others stayed silent.
>
> Two more desertions yesterday. It's as bad for the enemy. We're picking them up more and more now, as the weather worsens. Unshaven wretches with grey faces and pink eyelids, who think we must have cornered the supplies. But we all look like that.
>
> Things teeter on a whetted knife-edge.
>
> Except for the peasants. They've already dug in nicely for the winter. As Yurovski said, You never see a peasant eat. And you never see a thin one.
>
> They frighten me more than the Germans. Their illiteracy.

Their utter and bestial benightedness. There's more darkness in their heads than on the far side of the moon. But what really makes you want to empty your gun is the way they look at the toe of their boot until you've gone past. Then you feel that look alighting on the back of your neck, at the soft part that lies between the tendons, just where that little untrimmed wisp of a pigtail grows on a child.

A sickle sharpened on a fieldstone, hour by hour for centuries: that's what they are. They've been here so long they think they'll outlast the world.

In the Notebooks there follows a draft poem, undated:

> This is the cutthroat, endless,
> attritional *zugzwang*:
> knights, rooks, bishops, even
> the blood-sick bemused White king
>
> gone to the bayonet, and *tsarina*,
> *tsarevich, tsarevni*, all so delicate
> a thornscratch might have been
> enough. Now pawns trudge mud
>
> to mindlessness, slewing up
> stolen field guns to defend or
> take an empty square.
> This morning, across cornfields
>
> hibernating like a bear,
> beyond the road of dirtied
> slush we make daily to nowhere,
> calming the eye, lay snow
>
> illimitable (...)
>
> ~~as if whiteness~~
> ~~ever outlasted Springtime's~~ ... [indecipherable]
>
> ~~The white Red blood~~
> ~~has had to melt~~ (...)

These verses may require one or two brief comments.

Zugzwang, a rather more recondite metaphor from chess, is a technical term for a forced but disadvantageous position. Bal seems here to be thinking of a protracted endgame struggle, if one of inevitable issue.

Bal's draft refers to the Tsar, Nicholas the Second, as "blood-sick", and the entire family as "all so delicate/ a thornscratch might have been/ enough". In fact only Alexei, the thirteen-year old Tsarevich, was haemophilic, an inheritance from his mother's side. On July 16, 1918, Tsar and Tsarina, the sick Tsarevich and the four Tsarevni (together with their maidservants and the boy's doctor) were murdered in brutal, impromptu fashion by their Red guards, in a cellar in Ekaterinburg (now Sverdlovsk).

Gubski's critical censure of the banal chess metaphor operating in the beginning of Bal's poem 'Black Smoke' might equally be applied to these lines in draft – though Bal's stanzas here, after all, represent little more than a jotted-down sketch of a poetic idea, a provisional thought caught on the wing, not always even legible.

This unfinished poem has been included here, however, since some significance may be drawn precisely from the text's incompleteness, particularly from those final deletions in the manuscript. Do these represent cancellations of any tendentiousness in the poem, prior to its abrupt and presumably final abandonment?

Most of Bal's Civil War poems were in fact written in the late 'Twenties. But one can suggest that it is at this exact point, as early as 1919 and in a suppressed and not even fully-developed draft, that Bal is already beginning to define these later poems not only by what they will be but by what they will *not*, and by what he has no intention of their becoming, whatever his commitment to Bolshevism at this time. This draft's incompletion, its tailing away into silence in the face of its own suddenly overblown rhetoric ("The white Red blood/ has had to melt ..."), already seems to indicate Bal's refusal of histrionic or didactic heroism in his poetry.

It is probably for this reason – his eschewing of some tacit but increasingly 'official' line, openly glorifactory where it concerns the Red Army's part in the Civil War – that Bal's later poems on the subject are not to be published.

It is by dint of such minor decisions in working texts – by a single word added, or a line crossed out – that careers are made and fates are sealed.

6

An Education in the Classics

A note of Gubski's suggests that Bal's image of the Greek vase in the poem 'Black Smoke' may echo Keats' 'Ode On A Grecian Urn'. (Bal studied both Classics and English Literature when at university in St Petersburg.)

However, a page from Bal's Notebooks for the early period of the Civil War also makes reference to a more direct experience out of which, eventually, this poem grew:

> August 19, 1918. I will write this down, if only to stop seeing it before my eyes.
>
> A mother, grandmother and daughter – probably no more than fourteen years of age – whom we found gang-raped (no doubt was possible) then bayoneted upon the same hut floor.
>
> Some misbegotten hamlet I don't even know the name of because it wasn't on our maps.
>
> "Bastards," Zubatov said when we showed him. "Bastards." He looked hard at the daylight in the open door and took his breath in. But his voice still broke when he spoke. "They didn't even leave them open eyes to weep with," he said.
>
> A little later, as we were moving out, he looked across at me. "You'll get used to rooms like that," he said.
>
> All I know is we must still be green as grass. Because afterwards the three of us who'd gone into that hut couldn't even speak of it between ourselves. And I realised we were embarrassed or shamefaced in each other's sight. As if we were guilty for having seen it, or maybe just for being men.
>
> Whites, everyone assumes, or Germans. They were in the area. But who will ever know? Anything is possible for anyone, either to suffer or to get away with, in this filthiest of all possible wars. Every band of five men with a gun or a horse between them, Red, White, Grey or otherwise, are a law unto themselves. And at the moment that's the only rule of law

there is.

Aug. 20. I kept thinking afterwards of the lordly jokes the Greeks made about Zeus's satyriasis. Iope having to change into a cow to get away from him. Daphne into a laurel tree. That stuff won't work now, not any more. Not when it's happening daily somewhere. And, as with all the untaken prisoners, no witnesses are ever left. Even if you could work the miracle, it wouldn't be enough now. Men like these men would have hacked the tree down, slaughtered the cow. That's what this war is over anyway. Cows, and parcelled ground. They always counted for more than women did in that world.

7

Russian Roulette

The Red Army was often desperately short of ammunition during the Civil War, and it can be assumed that the "five bullets" Bal specifies in his poem 'Toy Soldier' refer to shortages, the "universe of scarcity" Dolgushin stares bitterly out into.

However, Bal explained this detail more fully in response to one of Gubski's questions. The Red soldiers were of course issued with standard six-chamber revolvers. But many of the guns were old-fashioned and in poor condition. "I used to lie awake dreaming of the blue Colt I would one day capture," Bal told Gubski. One day, as he had just finished reloading it, Bal's revolver fell from his hands in the mess-tent. As the butt struck the toe of his left boot the gun fired. The bullet shattered a just-rinsed plate which an orderly, as Bal described it, was holding out "like a target in a sideshow" so as to stand it in the rack to drain.

"Comedy," Bal went on to say, "is only the arbitrary hairsbreadth avoidance of a principle of arbitrary disaster. The wing of the angel of death, silent as a hunting owl's, its claws as sudden and as penetrating, hovers over every circus tumble. What we roar with is not laughter but vicarious relief."

For some time afterwards, Bal said, unless the revolver was likely to be in immediate use, he was in the habit of loading it with only five bullets, leaving the chamber first to the hammer empty.

But for the remainder of the Civil War, he added, he carried about with him, as a talisman, in one pocket or another, a fragment of the shattered plate.

"We all carried a piece of it, all of us who were in that tent. We were going to meet when the war was over, and fit that plate together again, and then get drunk. That was the idea anyway." Bal laughed at the absurdity of this. "In those days even non-combatants, people trying to live quietly at home in some godforsaken village, didn't know from one day to the next or between morning and night if they'd find their own houses or wives or parents or children still standing the next time they saw them. Life wasn't just in pieces in those days. It was being ground finer than sand. But you know how superstitious soldiers are. I suppose we thought we were placating Providence with a plan like that. Anyway," Bal said, "I still have my little piece of the plate. But of course the plate is still in pieces."

"A year later that bullet finally found me," Bal told Gubski. "Though at least it missed my head and heart. It even missed my left toe. It caught me just beside the point of the left knee. The bone was completely shattered.

"The boy who had been holding the plate wasn't so lucky. After that, he must have thought he was doomed to get home alive. But of course, as it happens he was killed a few days later. He was hit by a shell fragment. Though it wasn't that which killed him. What killed him was going under the wheel of the Lanchester armoured car as he fell, which just goes to show that there is such a thing as accidental death, even in war. When we sat him up the blood came out of his mouth like floodwater from an outfall pipe."

"What I suppose I'm trying to say," Bal told Gubski finally, "is that you look for a pattern in all these things, some higher meaning. Until you realise that there's only one meaning and it's this: that's how things are for us. We're one of those generations. We weren't born in a bed just so that we could die in one."

8

How It Was Done in the Don Basin

An extract from Bal's Notebooks gives the germ of other details in his poem 'Toy Soldier':

November 3 [1919]. Voloshin is from the Don Basin. A hard case, as they say. A miner before the Revolution. Afterwards he was in the Polish campaign. I don't know how he ended up with us. Anyway, an out and out Bolshevik. No disciplinary problems from the likes of him. Not even the usual soldier's complaints. "Don't start grumbling yet," he told Karpovsky the other evening. "Or what will you do later?"

"This is only the beginning," he said. "The Revolution didn't end with someone shitting in the Tsar's bed in the Winter Palace, or coming all over the Tsarina's frilly pillow. And that's how we have to see it. Not the end of history, as Comrade Marx would say. Its beginning. We were always clear about that. At least, in the Don Basin we were. That it was history we were making. We knew that. All of us. Out of our own blood and hair and skin."

When he talks, you can see where's he's picked up a few phrases here and there in Party meetings. But behind those is something harder than the coal he used to dig out with a pick. Perhaps we are creating a new breed of intellectuals. Uneducated people like Voloshin. But who can spell out their own lives as if for the first time, as they say it, like Adam naming plants and animals.

Voloshin looked slowly around the circle, at the rest of us. We were all listening now. Though we were all so wet and tired anybody could have held the floor.

"We were nothing before, most of us," he said. "You go down a mine some time. You'll learn what tiredness is. Before the Revolution we weren't even worth the weight of our own flesh. It's a funny thing, a man's life can be the lightest thing there is. It's not even the weight of a bullet. Yet a dead man is the heaviest thing you'll ever have to carry. Deadweight is right. I ought to know. I've seen a hundred. I must have shifted dozens. I've brought them up into the light. I've buried them. I've even used them as a barricade when I had to, like a sandbag. A thing to take a bullet meant for me. Sometimes that's all a man is worth to you: a sandbag." He spat into the fire. "I ought to know," he said. "I've left mates all over Poland. And enemies." He nodded, laughed, and looked slyly up at us. "Maybe even the odd bastard."

Naturally we all laughed at that, as if we knew about such things. Not to say that we haven't heard it all before. It's one of the myths of soldiering, so old it's got shells and fishbones in it. What it really says is: To the victors go the spoils. Just keep telling the troops that. So that the younger men, who don't yet know the smell of cunt from sour cream, as Zubatov always harangues us, will have something to look forward to, because we're warriors: the passionate love of Polish women. Even if we haven't most of us managed to find a Russian girl who will lie down and turn towards us yet.

I mustn't even begin to think about Marina. Not in that way. Even though it's the only way I can, sometimes. One thing I have come to understand is what a pious hypocrite I am. I despise Suslov and the others for the way they talk about women, their own wives even, as if they were whores. But although I'd never breathe her name out in their company, that's how I see her, use her, sometimes in my mind of minds.

And who am I to judge Suslov, or his wife? What do I know of marriage and home life in the shanty-towns, that huge *shtetl* of mud and typhus ringing holy Moscow? That's all poor swine like Suslov have ever known. Like Yurovski said (though he was talking about the Kiev hunger), a place where the rats eat babies.

Another 'Yurovski', on a Jewish prostitute: "Why not? What does it matter to me? They're all pink inside."

To a soldier, far from home or even from an oil lamp on a table with a cloth, that can become a truth of war.

★

[Bal has added to the foregoing manuscript an obviously later comment, in pencil, after the reference to Adam: "Only God knows what Shklovsky or Jakobson would make of such a scholastic simile. But let it stand as a moral warning on the dangers of the apophthegmatic form".]

Nov. 7. Today Voloshin started to tell us about the campaign in Poland. The terrible things done by both sides.

No time now. But someone must write all this down, talk to people like V.

A project. Start making a collection of sayings, anecdotes. History out of the mouths of common men. Sometimes a kind of poetry, even. "You are born in a clear field. But you die in a dark wood," V. said today. A proverb, of course. Probably as old as the hills. I've heard it before, long ago, when I was a child. But such force, such finality, the way V. said it. And then he got up and went, as if there was no more to be said. And there wasn't. That was his epitaph for them all, for all the things he had seen done.

Tolstoy knew all this, but he thought it was only worth talking to the peasants. But Villon knew it too, a city boy. *Sur le noel, morte saison, que les loups se vivent de vent.* When wolves live off the wind. Poets would give their back teeth for lines like that. Even Yesenin.

The point being that everyone in this war has a story to tell. Every deserter, every Jew. The murdered and the living. Even the horses have seen things that would astonish God. Only they can't talk.

But few of us, educated or not, can talk with the slow and ungainsayable authority of Voloshin, with those Tartar eyes and his skull still blue from headlice and his beard of iron filings.

9

Internal Exile of the Houseplant

The Union of Soviet Writers was established at the First Congress of Soviet Writers, which took place in the Hall of Columns of Moscow's House of Unions in August 1934. In his poem 'The Writers' Union Building, Moscow, 1937', Bal however, may be describing one of the Union's residential buildings ("Free hotel...?") – possibly Herzen House, on Tverskoi Boulevard, where he is known to have stayed when working on film scripts in Moscow in 1923.

During the 1920s, when the Union of Writers had been still a genuine professional organisation and not an instrument of State control, Bal had stayed in several of the Union's residential facilities, in Moscow and elsewhere, including apparently a holiday villa on the Black Sea. After the 1934 Congress, Bal, like many other writers, saw such privileges quickly disappear. A draft poem he evidently wrote in his first period of internal exile (probably in 1936) looks back on this earlier time:

Geranium

I stand in the single
window of this distant room,
the alternating hemispheres of
day and night passing

over me, quick as
clouds across a summer field.
I'm like ~~a houseplant~~ a red geranium
~~dying of neglect~~
neglected on a sill

while everyone is away.
(They're at the Black Sea,
drinking good red Georgian wine
like in the good old days

before I spilled the ink
over my copybook, not to
mention the blood, blood
Red and White I'd seen

lost into the ground
and blooming through rags
and cracking in
the lines of grimaces ...

All years ago ... But it's still
summer at the writers' villa
in Odessa, and the seaward
window fills with cloud

and glasses click down
on the tabletop, as in the days
before they tore the face out
of my passport ...)

Now I shrivel in this
window like a parched plant, hearing
the hiss of night rain
behind the pane of

memories, worthless fantasies.
This will not be enough, I
drill myself, ~~murmuri[ng]~~ moving dry lips
like a peasant learning

how to read. The life that was
or could have been is
over now. You must, I tell myself,
live slow and sure and silent

and within yourself. Act
blind and deaf and
dumb. Above all, dumb.
Shape words, bur give forth

> silence. Put out neither
> fruit nor flower nor leaf.
> You must look like a stone,
> but live. Live like a cactus.

This poem is written in Bal's notebook in purple ink. Underneath Bal has added in pencil – and in such a way that it is not clear if it is a prose afterthought about the poem or a new last line for it:

> Not even that. The lichen on a rock.

As it turns out not even silence is enough to guarantee survival. But for Bal, as for other writers in the Soviet Union during the Thirties, silence seems to represent the last integrity possible – preferable, at any rate, to a compromised existence as a publishing writer in a world where only what is tailored to be acceptable to the State is ever found to be so.

When Y.N. Gubski asks him in 1937 why he now publishes so little Bal replies, with a certain ingenuousness, that he has always written sparingly and throws away many poems.

"What do you want me to say? A real poet, after all, can be judged by the poems he rejects or abandons just as much as by those he chooses or is lucky enough to find a publisher for. Before he even thinks of submitting his work to the editor of a State publishing house, a poet has to pass his own work through the eye of a needle. Which is itself, or ought to be, a hard gate to pass. As it is for the camel in the old story."

Bal went on: "When you come to think of it, a poet is something like a camel. Don't you agree? Not because of how much he can carry on his back, I don't mean that. But because he can live on his own water for long periods, if need be. When you're crossing a desert, it's not a matter of how much you can carry – how many books, say, or how big they are – but of how much water you can store. I'm like that kind of camel. And that desert is my present silence."

Bal's use of the Biblical parable here can be seen as both evasive and provocative. Its major proposition, of course, merely affirms the artistic principle that it is as difficult for a serious poet to write a poem which satisfies himself – to consign even a good poem to its own completion – as it is for "a camel to pass through the eye of a needle". As Paul Valéry was to put it: "A poem is never finished. It is only abandoned."

However, a further, ironic parallel seems to be invited between the rich man's difficulty in gaining "the Kingdom of Heaven" and that of *the real poet* in catching the eye of an editor at a State publishing house.

It is also impossible not to infer a veiled criticism of certain otherwriters from Bal's insistence on a poet's own creative autonomy and self-critical sense – principles which (as will be seen later in these Notes) are also expressed, though in much more obviously dangerous circumstances, by the short-story writer Isaac Babel. In a period when officially favoured writers were only too happy to be paid on quantity or sheer bulk, even a too-insistent concern for literary quality could appear as a subversive form of individualism.

Bal's view of some of his contemporaries may be gauged from a satirical fragment in the Notebook at this time:

The Muscle Under the Tongue

Poets? Writers? Hardly.
But there's no surer way to fame
for camp dogs: licking the hand
that feeds them space
to do so, prints their name.

10

Stalin's Wings

Bal's poem 'The Leader' makes reference to two buildings, the Palace of the Soviets and the Moskva Hotel. Since the poem was written (probably in about 1935) the architectural history of Moscow has served only to increase any dimension of irony in these allusions to the building programme of the Stalin years.

    The Palace of Soviets was intended to be the ultimate statement of megalomania in public building. The largest architectural structure in the world, it was to be built in honour of Stalin's first Five Year Plan, and to accommodate Party Congresses, meetings of the Supreme Soviet, etc. Besides a vast number of offices, it would also contain restaurants and other amenities, and two huge halls with seating for 20,000 and 8,000 respectively. Situated within view of the Kremlin, on the site of the demolished Cathedral of the Redeemer, its ground area was 110,000 square metres. The cement used in the foundations amounted to sixteen per cent of the annual output of the Soviet Union. The projected central section was to be a quintuple-tiered skyscraper tower surmounted by a massive statue representing the liberated proletariat. This was later replaced by a plan for a statue of Lenin, the dimensions of which were to be enlarged from the original eighteen metres to seventy-five metres in height, the entire palace acting as a pedestal for this gigantic statue. After several years of revision to the plans, it was intended that building would start on January 1st, 1935, but it was not until 1937 that final changes were accepted. Early in the construction work a major difficulty with water seepage arose, as might be expected in a low site so close to the river. The base was covered with bitumen in a futile attempt to counteract this problem. Nevertheless, by 1941 the huge steel skeleton of the building began to rise above the city. Now, however, it was the wartime emergency, coupled with the increasingly insoluble problem of the insecure foundation, which suspended the work, though the plans for the building were never officially abandoned. As war continued, the shortage of steel led to the skeleton being gradually dismantled, piece by piece, for use in the war effort. In 1960 a swimming pool was constructed over the foundations of the intended palace.

The Moskva Hotel is an impressive if somewhat monumental edifice of granite and concrete on Moscow's Okhotny Ryad. Designed by the architects A.V. Shchusev, L.I. Savelyev and O.A. Stapran, it was completed in 1935. Despite its imposing portico and piers, which dwarf passers-by in the street below, the facade of the building has come to represent a grim joke in that the left and right wings of its frontage – each twelve storeys high – are completely different in design and look mismatched. Apparently Stalin was shown a plan in which the front elevation offered two variants in juxtaposition. Failing to notice this, Stalin approved the plan as it stood. No one dared point out the error, and the building was completed to incorporate both designs.

11

Mandelstam's Bird

It is not certain if Bal and Mandelstam knew each other personally. But when Gubski interviewed him in the spring of 1937, Bal spoke of the other poet at length, and described how he had first encountered him at a public reading Mandelstam gave in Leningrad in 1933.

"The gossip about Mandelstam wasn't very favourable at that time," Bal told Gubski. "The general feeling was he was something of a reactionary, and was finished as a poet anyway. I seem to remember that he'd been accused of plagiarism over some translation or other. You know the kind of thing. Anyway, I suppose I'd better admit I knew him more through this reputation than through his poems. I don't read a great deal of poetry, I never have. And he wasn't a well-known poet, anyway. He still isn't. He probably never will be. Also, for me he was a type. One of the older generation. One of those who'd sat in their apartments all through the Revolution and the Civil War, grumbling about having to burn the furniture, and waiting to see what happened. All this while we had changed the world. Now we were going to change poetry. This, at any rate, was what I thought.

"Anyway, I went along to the reading. There was another poet reading that evening whom I did want to hear.

"I remember that I was abstracted that night. It doesn't matter why. Not any more. Just say I had something on my mind. Nothing important, as it would seem now. Or say that, like Count Vronsky, I had toothache, and I couldn't think of anything but that.

"Whatever the reason, it was of more concern to me on that particular night than this particular failed poet's work. You know how it is. Sometimes you're watching one thing and thinking about another.

"In spite of this, I couldn't help noticing a certain hostility in the hall towards Mandelstam, when it came to his turn to read. Mutterings at some of the poems. Shuffling feet.

Someone even made what I suppose you could politely call a scathing comment, a single word, but loud enough for it to have been heard everywhere in the hall, not to mention on the platform. It was only later I understood that all of this must have been orchestrated by his enemies, let's call them. Just as the gossip about him had been, and the things that Zaslavski and others had been saying about him in print. Also, Mandelstam read – how can I put it? – very curtly, even arrogantly, you might say, as if he knew enough to hope for nothing from this audience. He was right, in that. As I said, no sooner had he got to his feet than the mutterings and throat-clearings started. But in fact, Mandelstam's dismissive manner was only increased by all this. Which probably helped turn even neutral sections of the audience against him.

"Mandelstam was a small man with a big head, to put it bluntly. It was only when he stood up to read that you saw how short he was. Seated he looked bigger than he actually was. Like Homer says somewhere, about Odysseus.

"Anyway, all through this my mind was somewhere else. Like just about everyone else's in that noisy audience, it seemed, I was only sitting there, waiting for this reading to be over, not really listening to that little man up on the platform.

"But as he kept reading, almost in defiance of us, I think, a strange thing happened, for me at least. I can only explain it by saying that it was like something that has occasionally happened to me at concerts: you can sit through three quarters of the programme trying to look as if you're listening to the music but in all truth faintly bored, wishing it would finish so you can light a cigarette, get a drink in the bar, have a chat with your friends. When suddenly one piece, or even a single movement, comes through to you – in a way it never does over the radio – with such clarity and power that it overwhelms you. It's as if suddenly your powers of musical understanding and sheer concentration are so great that this piece seems to exist not just up there on the platform but is welling up inside you, and you realise with a pang of admiration, even envy, what it must be to have written a piece like that, or even to be capable of playing it.

"Victor Shklovsky told me some time afterwards that Mandelstam carries his poems about for a long time before he even puts a word on paper. But, as Shklovsky said, they weigh a lot at birth.

"When Mandelstam finished reading there was a silence. Some people clapped politely. But this was almost drowned by the noise of other people standing, complaining, pushing their chairs back. I found myself on my feet, clapping and staring, furiously almost, at that little man who was now seated again with a hooded gaze, a look of contemptuous indifference on his face. I knew how hurt he was, and how hopeless he realised things were. There were tears in my eyes. 'Real tears', as my brother Jacob used to say of his children when they were babies."

Bal's later familiarity with Mandelstam's work is clear from several allusions in his poem 'For Osip Emilievich Mandelstam'. This use of direct reference or quotation of another poet's work is in the first instance, doubtless, an homage. In another sense, however, its essence may have been consciously 'preservative' or 'mnemonic': the invocation and celebration, by accurate reference, of what may be in danger of disappearance. Thus Bal's poem quotes from Mandelstam's 1928 story 'The Old Woman's Bird', published in the collection *The Noise of Time*. The reference to the goldfinch, in particular, directs the reader to one of Mandelstam's greatest poems:

> Goldfinch of mine, I'll cock my head;
> together we'll view the world:
> winter day, jagged as stubble,
> is it as harsh to your eye as to mine?
>
> Tail, a little black and yellow boat.
> Head dipped in colour past the beak.
> Goldfinch, do you know you're a goldfinch?
> Do you know how much?
>
> What are things like behind his forehead?
> Black. Red. Yellow. White.
> One eye on things both ways. Now he's stopped
> looking, and flown from between them.

This poem was written in December, 1936, during Mandelstam's period of internal exile in Voronezh. It is therefore of interest that Bal referred to it during his conversation with Gubski in the summer of 1937 – though it is doubtful now whether either scholarship or chance will determine how a copy of Mandelstam's poem – which of course was not published in the Soviet Union – came into Bal's possession at this time.

The following is again taken from Gubski's account of the meeting with Bal at which Mandelstam was discussed:

> The conversation got back to Mandelstam. Bal looked at me shrewdly for a second as if he was considering whether or not to do something. I looked back at him. He'd agreed to my coming here. He had no one else to say these things to. Bal got up and took a loose piece of paper from a book and read it to me. It was a poem of Mandelstam's about a goldfinch. It was one I hadn't come across before.
>
> "It's not an important poem for these times," Bal said when he'd finished. "It's not about oil or economic plans or the Moscow subway. It's just about watching a bird."
>
> Bal shrugged and put aside the piece of the paper with the poem on it. I didn't like to ask him if I could read it for myself yet. He lit a cigarette – he was a heavy smoker – and leaned back in his chair.
>
> "One day," he said, "Mandelstam will fly out from between his poems for ever, as the bird flies from between its own eyes. Not your eyes. Not mine. Not even Mandelstam's. Its own. But like the bird, Mandelstam will leave a poem on the branch. No one will alter that."
>
> I said nothing. I knew he wanted to talk.
>
> "It's the bird's going," Bal said eventually, "which proves its freedom. Which is something every birdwatcher knows. That bird's not a stuffed bird. It isn't a vulture in a case."
>
> He gestured sideways in a way I understood to carry right across the city to the Writers' Club. I think Bal always felt safe criticising those bastards to me because he knew they'd just turned down my membership again.
>
> He picked up the sheet of paper with the poem on it again, and now he passed it across to me to read.
>
> "On first hearing you probably thought it was about a bird," he said. "Now read the poem again."

12

The Moscow Reckoning

Bal's admiration for, and familiarity with, Isaac Babel's work is obvious from his poem, 'For Isaac Emanuelovich Babel'. And, as in the poem dedicated to Mandelstam, this familiarity lends itself to specific literary allusion and even direct quotation. Detail concerning the Jewish cemetery at Kozin, for example, invokes Babel's terse, masterly prose sketch of that title in his Civil War stories *Red Cavalry*, which had been published in a collected volume in 1932. Some of Babel's earlier, more journalistic work provides the source for the section concerning the Palace of Motherhood established in Moscow in the immediate post-Revolutionary period: in 1918 Babel had published two articles ('Premature Babies' and 'The Palace of Motherhood') in Gorky's journal *Novaya zhizn* (New Life).

But perhaps the poem's most telling references are to oral statements Babel had made about his life and work several year previously, at the 1934 Writers' Congress, where he was one of the speakers. (Was Bal present in the audience on this occasion?) It was at this time, and in order to forestall or accomodate criticism over his 'lack of productivity' since the *Red Cavalry* stories, that Babel referred to himself sardonically as the master of a 'new' literary genre, which he had himself invented: he was, he said, "the master of the genre of silence".

Given the already growing climate of fear and conformism at this time, this was a brave attempt at irony. Babel went on to talk about the respect for a reader every writer needs, and how real respect for the reader consists in giving him something "surprising", something other than a "certified genuine copy" of daily life. Art, he said, feeds on unexpectedness. The unacceptability of this literary principle may be measured from the fact that it was at this same Congress that Andrei Zhdanov, Stalin's cultural commissar and son-in-law, first promulgated 'socialist realism' as the official literary style, i.e. a mode of writing from which all unexpectedness had been specifically proscribed. It must have been clear to everyone in his audience exactly why 'silence' had become such a grimly logical necessity for Babel, the admirer of Maupassant and the master of laconic brevity in Russian prose, who had indeed once written (to quote his celebrated dictum correctly): "No steel can pierce the human heart so chillingly as a full stop at the right moment"

But what also underlies Bal's 1937 poem – and probably occasioned it – are further public statements concerning his work that Babel was compelled to make on September 28th, 1937, at the Writers' Union in Moscow, an event which Bal evidently attended. This public interview was arranged by the magazine *Literaturnaya ucheba* (Learning To Write), though in fact it was not published in the Soviet Union until 1964, when it appeared in the Moscow quarterly *Nash sovremennik* (Our Contemporary). It is important to bear in mind the context of this second interview. In the autumn of 1937 the Yezhov terror is already beginning and the least indiscretion could be fatal. But, as Babel's daughter Nathalie has pointed out, "it was just as dangerous to refuse an interview as give one. In trying to be both truthful and prudent, Babel was forced to steer a careful course when touching on sensitive issues."

One subject on which Babel's celebrated 'silence' needed to be particularly strategic was that of certain current stories he had written on the problematical theme of collectivisation. ('Gapa Guzhva' and 'Kolyvushka' are the only two of these stories to survive; to date, neither has been published in the Soviet Union.) Another reason for his 'silence', however, was the simple difficulty of getting his work into print at this time. A number of stories, despite Gorky's recommendation, had recently been dropped from the anthology *God shesmadtsaty* (The Sixteenth Year) – which, as the commemorative title indicates, was an important anthology, if only as an index as to which writers were now sufficiently in favour as to be allowed to commemorate the post-Revolutionary process to that date. Moreover, Babel's play 'Maria' had been cancelled while still in rehearsals at the Vakhtangov theatre in Moscow. The signs were already ominous, in fact. Obviously these events did not, however, represent explanations that Babel could adduce in public for his recent lack of publication.

On the other hand, Babel's own sporadic and limited output was well known. As Nathalie Babel describes it, his "compulsion to rewrite, to produce endless variants – compounded by an increasing reluctance to part with his manuscripts until they met his own exacting standards – had plagued him since the beginning of his career". There are, then, in this sense, good (as well as bad) reasons why Babel chooses to speak of his silence in terms of his customary working method rather than the closing down of opportunites for him to publish. The following are extracts from the transcription of the interview:

> "*Interviewer*: Readers are puzzled by your rather lengthy silence.
> *Babel*: It puzzles me too, so in this respect there's not much difference between us.
>
> To tell the honest truth, I'm simply not very well equipped to do this job. And I wouldn't do it if I felt I'd be better off doing something else. But this is the only job that, with a great deal of hard work, I can do more or less properly. That's the first thing. In the second place, I have a highly-developed critical sense. Third, we live in stormy, revolutionary times, and I'm one of those people who are not so much concerned with the word 'what'. I'm quick to feel admiration, hatred or sorrow. Some comrades, when they feel these things, immediately rush to get it all down on paper. And if they're accomplished journalists, or they're good at writing odes or satires, sometimes it turns out very well. But by temperament I'm always interested in the 'how' and the 'why'. These questions need careful thought and study, and you have to approach the business of writing with great honesty in order to answer them in literary form. That's how I explain it to myself ..."

Babel returns to the subject later in the interview:

> "You talk about my silence. I'll let you in on a secret. I've wasted several years trying, with due allowance for my own tastes, to write things at length, with a lot of detail and philosophy – striving for the sort of truth I've been talking about. It didn't work out with me. So, although I'm an admirer of Tolstoy's, in order to achieve something I have to work in a way that's the opposite of his.
>
> "Let me put it this way: the point is that Tolstoy was able to describe what happened to him minute by minute, he remembered all of it. Whereas I, obviously, only have it in me to describe the most interesting five minutes I've experienced out of the last twenty-four hours. This has to be the reason.

Interviewer: So Tolstoy ran to 23 hours and 55 minutes longer than you?

Babel: Well, now, self-depreciation is just not in my nature. And if I wanted to make my life a misery by wondering who writes better, Tolstoy or I – even supposing I reached the conclusion *he* did – I'd probably loathe and detest him.

"But since we're here under the auspices of 'Learning to Write', and can talk about the tricks of the trade, I've told you why I can manage the short things but not the long ones. However, to forestall the slightest suggestion that I'm running myself down, I should add that many of my comrades, even though their stock of interesting facts and observations is no larger than mine, nevertheless write them up in true 'Tolstoyan' fashion. What this results in is known to all their victims."

Babel ends the interview by returning to his own work, again in such a way as to carry an implicit critique of some of his contemporaries:

"I think the things I have written could have been better, simpler. But I was one of those people who in their youth accept pimples as natural. I might be wrong, perhaps I'm blinded by conceit, but I think I see what I want to say and how to say it better now than I did then, when I wrote those things. The only cause I've got for satisfaction is that I don't have to take back anything I have written."

Given the difficulties, and risks, inherent for him in this conversation, Babel's skill in defending himself and his work is remarkable. His answers throughout the entire interview represent a masterpiece of cautious irony and ambiguity, and can be interpreted in total as a subtle but principled indictment of some of his officially-favoured contemporaries in Soviet literature. Babel's silence – like the spare, lapidary style he is defending – must be contrasted with the turgid piecework 'productivity' of certain writers (some of them must have been in the audience on this occasion) who were only too pleased ro receive a regular pay on wordage.

"It was all very politely conducted," Bal told Gubski, in reference to Babel's interview. "After all, Babel was a famous writer, one of Gorky's protégés. And the old man was still known to think highly of him. But as I listened to Babel talk I felt this indescribable tension. There was this unbelievable exhilaration simply at what he was doing. The way he managed to damn Sholokov, the official blue-eyed boy, with a kind of offhand praise. 'Progressing along the right lines,' he said judiciously, like you'd say to the parent of some sedulous pupil in a term report. Not to mention the reference to 'Tolstoyans' and their victims. And the way he stood up for a poor, despised drunk like Yuri Olesha, whom they'd been harrying for years. 'A major writer,' he said. Which he obviously is.

"But it wasn't just the way he took that hack of an interviewer on.

It was what he was saying. As if it was not too late to believe that a brave man, and a great writer, trying to speak the truth for himself, could still be listened to. As if his words from that platform could still have the power they always had for me in every page he wrote.

"But underneath all this, which was an uncontrollable urge to get up from my seat and cheer, scream out 'Yes, that's it, that's absolutely right!' – uncontrollable in every sense except that of course I managed to control it, and sat quietly like everybody else – underneath all this, my blood ran cold for him. It ran cold for myself. For all of us. The way molten lead quite suddenly seems almost to freeze to a bullet in the mould.

"I remember that from where I sat, as he moved his head, the lights kept glinting like moons off those round glasses he wore.

"Afterwards I happened to see him coming down some steps inside the building. He was alone. He looked drained, empty. I thought it was a look I'd seen on soldiers at the front. After an attack, or sometimes just from sheer exhaustion, you'd suddenly notice that a man looked like a corpse. As if he were already dead. 'He's gone,' we used to say. 'He's just waiting to stiffen up.' Babel would know what I mean by that. But, for Babel, I knew that the bullet was already hardening, and had his name on it."

(At this juncture Gubski notes that Bal lights a fifth cigarette from the fourth.)

"But it's bad luck to talk like that," Bal said. "To someone or other, we might all have that look these days. Even Gorky. And probably some of the soldiers I saw like that came out of the war without losing a tooth or a fingernail or the pus out of a boil. They ate a spoonful of food and woke up again, and in the end even survived."

Isaac Babel didn't. Shortly after his speech at the Writers' Union he was arrested. He is presumed to have died, in unrecorded circumstances, in a concentration camp, in 1939 or '40.

Babel's short stories have remained only 'selectively' available in the Soviet Union. It is only now in 1988, under the policy of *glasnost*, that the Union of Soviet Writers is to publish, in two volumes, a complete and definitive edition of his work.

13

Editorial Reminiscences

In 1938 or '39 Yevgeni Nikolayevich Gubski submitted, under his own name, Victor Bal's poem 'The Galley' to the Leningrad literary periodical *Zurnal*. The poem was received and read by Aleksandr Stepanov, then a young literary editor for the magazine. He returned the manuscript by post with a standard typed rejection slip, signed by himself, but making no comment on the poem. After Gubski's death the opened envelope, the poem (with the words "by Y.N. Gubski" following the title) and the rejection slip were found among the other papers of Bal's which had been in his possession.

The following is the transcript of an interview with Stepanov which was recorded in his ward in the geriatric wing of a Leningrad hospital in April, 1987. It is a prolix, paradoxical, confessedly partial and, in at least one sense, initially prevaricatory account of events that had taken place almost fifty years earlier. Stepanov, who had recently passed his seventy-seventh birthday and undergone a gall-stone operation in the same week, seemed pale but remarkably alert. He spoke of the past without apparent effort of either speech or memory. Only occasionally did the light blue eyes wander and cloud or the dry, rasping voice falter or have to pause to clear itself.

Relevant sections of the interview are given here because of the light they may be thought to throw on Bal's life and on the general background.

> "Yes, I remember the poem. What's more to the point, I remembered it then. Literary editors have long memories for things like that. At least, this one does. I might not be able to tell you what I had for lunch yesterday, but things like that I don't forget. I knew this Gubski, and I knew he hadn't written this poem. I don't know whether Mikhail Alexandrovich Sholokov wrote *And Quietly Flows The Don* or whether he filched it out of some dead soldier's knapsack. Some people say he must have stolen it, he didn't have the talent in him for a book like that. I'm not saying this is true, you understand. But who knows? Anything's possible under conditions of war, and so on. Why stop at cutting off a dead finger for a wedding

ring, or digging a gold tooth from a head? In those days, after the First Writers' Congress, people would do anything, they'd fight like cornered rats, and not even for what you'd call a position or anything substantial, but just for a few inches in print, a sign of official favour. It was only once they had that that they felt safe.

"Naturally, it didn't work like that. You were probably better off not attracting attention at all. But there were no guarantees either way. That was the problem always. You never knew whether you'd gone too far or not done enough. No great writer ever agonised over a poem in the way certain writers did then, in some bureaucratic intrigue to get one of their own accepted. And that was true in every other area of life, nor just in writing. It was like walking around with a stone in your shoe: and that stone was the stone you thought you might have left unturned. You were scared to leave it unturned. But you were scared to turn it, too, in case someone noticed you doing it, or because you didn't know what you might find underneath it. Actually, it was in your head instead of in your shoe. But that tiny stone still crippled you after a while. That's why I think that for certain perfectly ordinary people arrest must have come as an unimaginable shock. But to others it must have been almost a kind of relief. Those of us who could see a little of what was going on were already aged with waiting for our turn.

"Anyway, I knew this Gubski, as I was saying, and I knew he hadn't written this poem he'd put his name to. Not because it was too good for him to have written, I don't mean that, though he had as little talent as most of us. No, the thing was that I knew I'd heard the poem before. I recognised the damn thing. They always tell you it's a small world. Leningrad's smaller still.

"When I came to think about it, to try to place it, I seemed to remember that it was Fyodor Voulitsky I'd heard read it one night. At a reading of young poets, unknowns mostly. Everybody and his girlfriend thought they were poets in those days. Even I did. [Laughs]

"I don't know what happened to Voulitsky. He wrote a few good poems. This was a long time ago. Before we all became pimps to power. I'm talking about the Twenties, now. But he wrote a few good poems. One or two.

"Now of course I know the poem was by Victor Bal. He read too, that evening. Not that I knew him then. This must have been 1924, '25. A long time ago.

"Anyway, aside from his bad luck in my elephantine memory, Gubski didn't even have the sense, or was just too plain desperate, to realise that this poem 'The Galley', no matter who'd written it, was the last kind of thing any magazine could have published at that time. People did sudden, ludicrous things in those days, acting blindly, out of pure desperation, or loss of nerve. I don't know when Bal wrote that poem. Probably even before the Revolution. But this was the late Thirties now, remember, 1938 or '9. That kind of poem, what it was saying, would have been absolutely unpublishable then. It was closer to the bone then than it would have been under the Tsar, or, come to that, Caesar himself. And, if that wasn't enough, a poem about a galley? [Laughs] We wanted poems that were up to date, about tractors or tanks. Comrade Stalin personally driving them, that was understood. Well, this is just literary gossip, as you know. But it's only now that we can say these things. At least, they tell us we can.

"I didn't even refer the poem upwards. I just put it in an envelope and sent it back. I did Gubski a good turn, you could say, though I don't suppose he ever thought so.

"What was Bal like? I didn't know him very well. He was a member of the Writers' Union, of course. But that didn't necessarily mean much, even that he was a writer. All I knew in those days was he was now doing film scripts, in Moscow. To be honest, I never particularly wanted to get to know him.

"What shall I say? He always had a lot to say for himself, I remember. And he had a kind of arrogance about him. He used to swan around Leningrad in a big wolfskin coat, it came right down to his ankles. Actually, I always thought he was something of a *poseur*.

"He came across once when I was entertaining some guests at the Writers' Club, and took the salt off the table, still talking back over his shoulder to the table he'd left. Not a word. Not even a Thank You. Let alone a May I Please? Just a half-raised eyebrow. Then he took the salt back to his own table and sat down again, still talking.

"As for that careful limp of his, I didn't believe in that for a minute. He used to forget to do it sometimes. I think it went with the wolfskin coat. Like they used to say where I come from about Orthodox Jews, 'If you can't fight wear a big hat'.

"I remember that his wife was very beautiful. But in a way that you didn't see straight off. You know the type: they seem unobtrusive till you really look at them. She always looked very calm, but shy. She wasn't a Jewish type at all. She looked more like a Finn.

"Then one day someone told me she was having an affair with this actor, or he might have been a singer. Anyway, something like that. I don't remember his name. And I suppose there must have been something in it, because I saw them together once, they came into this restaurant together. Actually, it was The Stray Dog, on Mikhailovskaya Square, of all places. They came in and everyone looked at them. Or at him, really. He had those kind of looks. When he walked into a room, people stopped talking and eating and looked at him, men as well as women. As I say, I don't remember his name. I don't think I ever knew it. I just remember him coming into that restaurant with her.

"I don't know what happened to him, or her. In those days it was difficult to keep track of your own life and death, let alone other people's extramarital affairs. I never saw either of them again, or heard anything about them.

"So probably, looks or not, he wasn't much of a singer or actor or whatever it was he was. In the end, I suppose, like most of us, he must have come to nothing."

13

Vronsky's Toothache

The cassette spool revolved silently on the Grundig machine. A nurse came through the ward. Stepanov began to speak of other subjects. At length he fell silent, as if he was tired and the interview was over now. Then briefly, abruptly, he returned to the story he had left a little while before:

"After all these years, it's hard to get out of the habit of lying. That's what it must be. But if you can't tell the truth, or at least your side of it, when you get to my age, you never will.

"That was nonsense, what I said earlier, about Voulitsky. I don't even know why I bothered to lie about that. I mean, thinking that the poem Gubski sent me was by him. What does any of this matter now? I knew the poem was by Bal. I'd heard him read it. I recognised it in the thirty seconds it might have taken me to read it through.

"All of this comes of a lifetime of having to make out that you know less than you do.

"Like the other things I didn't tell you. Like the man who came into the restaurant with Marina Bal. Do you want to know the name of Marina Bal's lover? His name was Koussevits. Konstantin Koussevits. He was an actor. I suppose you could say I made a point about finding out about him. I can even tell you the year this happened. It was 1933. Was it really more than fifty years ago? The speed of light I can believe. The hardest thing in the world to accept is the speed of time.

"I never knew what became of Koussevits. That part was true. I don't even know what became of Marina Bal. And her I was in love with. In the way you can be at twenty-three, without hope or speculation, with another man's wife, a man you don't even like.

"I was never envious of Victor Bal, not sexually. After all, he was her husband. A husband has certain rights. I never even thought about her in that way. I just used to love to watch her from the other side of the room. But I was jealous of

Koussevits. You won't believe this, but when I saw her come into the restaurant with him I felt it was me she was betraying. But I suppose it was only my idea of her. Because under the tablecloth I was suddenly as stiff for her as if I was Bal himself looking on. Jealousy, they say, is the greatest aphrodisiac of all.

"I suppose she's dead now. Gone into the world of light. And Koussevits. He was in some play at the Alexandrinski at the time. But I never heard of him again after that.

"But I remember that night. It was May. He wore an orange scarf. She was wearing a white dress. I remember the night because there was a poetry evening at the House of Arts. Normally I should have had to be there. But I made the decision to stay away because, well, one of the readers that night was to be Osip Mandelstam, and I knew there was going to be some kind of demonstration against him. Which meant he was as good as on the train, as we used to say later. Knowing this I, well, I suppose I didn't have the heart to go. I went to The Stray Dog and watched an awful cabaret and drank three bottles of wine instead.

"Despite this, even now I can remember everything as clearly as if the candle was still burning in that empty bottle on their table."

★ ★ ★

Out of all the past that is irrecoverable, it is one of the ironies of historical and biographical research that isolated facts or grounds for compelling supposition emerge, when they do, in so random and irrelevant a form.

Among these tiny, piecemeal discoveries out of a lost life and a time without records seems to be the reason for Victor Bal's preoccupation on the night he heard Mandelstam read.

All the Scattered Fragments

No one will ever mend
the little faceted tumbler

of Armenian brandy
you drained in one and

smashed in the empty hearth
that final afternoon

on Zubovsky Street:
only a crushed-glass grit

of too many toasts,
an undissolving salt,

is in your liver.
You won't find all

the pieces of
the napkined glass you

stood on at your wedding
till it broke:

the biggest sliver
worked its way

towards your heart.
The broken plate won't

fly back together again
or the dead get

smartly up off the floor
like gymnasts, in that

magical way things happen
in a film rewinding.

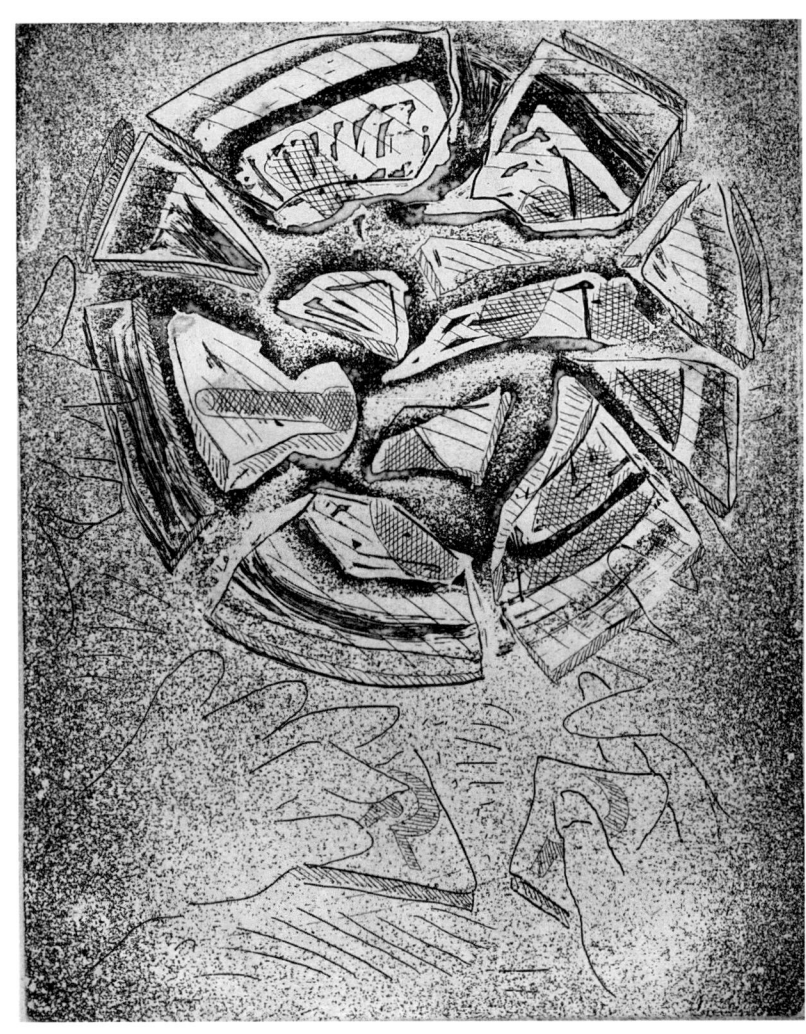

Acknowledgements

Some of these poems have appeared or will appear in *Poetry Wales, The Rialto, New England Review/Bread Loaf Quarterly, Label 8,* and *Picture: Welsh Poets*. Part of the textual material in this book was first 'published' (made public) at readings at the Willa Ichon in Bremen, and at the universities of Hannover, Kiel, Osnabrück and Oldenburg; at the Oriel Bookshop, Cardiff; during the 1987 Birmingham Arts Festival; at the University of East Anglia; and in a lecture on censorship during the 1988 World Development Conference at Atlantic College.

I am grateful to the British Council for travel grants which have advanced my sense of what this book would be.

This book above all acknowledges, and is dedicated to, the work and memory of those writers who knew they bore the seed-corn, and kept it dry.

The Authors

Duncan Bush was born in Cardiff in 1946, and educated at Warwick University, Duke University (USA) and Wadham College, Oxford.

His poetry, short fiction and translations have been widely published and have received a number of awards. His first three poetry collections, *Aquarium* (1983), *Salt* (1985) and *Masks* (1994) were all awarded the Welsh Arts Council Poetry Prize. Poems from *Aquarium*, *Salt* and *Black Faces, Red Mouths* were collected in *The Hook* (1997) and a further collection, *Midway*, appeared in 1998. A new collection, *The Trapeze Artist*, appears in 2012. Bush is also the author of two novels, *Glass Shot* (1991) and *Now All the Rage* (2008

Duncan Bush lives with his wife in Luxembourg. He is the co-editor of *The Amsterdam Review*.

John Selway was born in Askern, Yorks. in 1938, but moved to his parents' birthplace of Abertillery, Gwent, in 1940. He was a student at the Royal College of Art between 1959 and 1962, and lived for a year in Portugal. He taught for many years at Newport College of Art, where he met Duncan Bush and collaborated on *The Genre of Silence*.

John Selway's solo shows include Roland, Browse and Delbanco, Piccadilly Gallery and elsewhere. Group shows include Young Contemporaries, Café Royal Centenary Exhibition in 1965, Camden Arts Centre, South Wales Group, Welsh Arts Council and International Arts Fairs in Basle and Dusseldorf. Newport Museum and Art Gallery held an important retrospective in March-April 2007. Arts Council, Welsh Arts Council, National Museum of Wales in Cardiff and a number of provincial public galleries in Wales and England hold his work, as does Johannesburg Art Gallery, South Africa.